Prayer changes everything

The Stories

in

"My Little Book

of

Testimonies'

are true Stories.

***

This book is written so that you may read some of the things that I would like to share of what has happened by having God our Heavenly Father in my life since I was five years old..

It is good to look back sometimes and see what The Lord has done in our lives.
    It is incredible to think that He can use us to help others in different ways and that we can Pray directly to God through Jesus Christ His Son, who is our Lord and Saviour - also we have The Holy Spirit to help us to pray. (Especially when we are not sure how to!)

God waits to hear our prayers - however we do need to have invited Jesus into our heart and to have become a Christian for prayers to be effective.

My Testimony

This is to let you know that The Lord Jesus Christ
Healed my lungs of an incurable disease
in 1984 in Perth, Western Australia by the
laying on of hands at a Church
Service there.
Praise The Lord for His Healing Power
The same now as when Jesus walked upon the earth.
Also I have come to know The Holy Spirit
More fully in my life
Since inviting Him into my heart
So that the Lord God can use me
For His work and Glory.
The Holy Spirit is our Teacher,
Comforter also our Guide.
He wants us to fellowship with Him each day.
He is the one who helps us to pray.
His presence is lovely,
Once you have lived with The Holy Spirit
(who is The Spirit of Jesus Christ)
You will never want to live without Him.

Jesus said:

in

<u>John Chapter 14 verse 6.</u>

I am the Way

The Truth

and

the Life.

No one comes to the Father

except by me.

***

I will start writing about my Testimonies from when I was five years old about the things that I remember.

Hoping that they will be of interest to those who read them and that God will bless each person who kindly reads and believes. Amen.

<u>I was 2yrs. old when the 2nd world war started and 8yrs when it ended.</u>

5yrs old. - I invited Jesus into my life sitting out the front of our Church Sunday School at 'St. Lenard's' Hythe Hill, Colchester Essex. England.

The Sunday School children were asked to come out to sit at the front of the Church for a Story read by the Priest. Then we were asked to put our hand up if we would like to invite Jesus into our heart.

So I put my hand up and became a Christian.

***

My Mother and I lived with my Nanna Tainton in her house on Hythe Hill Colchester, while my father was in the Army (Second World War)

As the 5yr. old - I had Bronchial Pneumonia and was in Hospital - very ill. Penicillin had been invented so that saved my life. - Then I was at home to recover in bed for a long time. I Remember the heated Bread Poultice they put on my lungs each day to help heal them.

Nanna used to put them on, we could not always get the Kaolin so they made them with cloth putting bread inside and soaking them in hot water, cooling the poultice of course before wrapping around my chest.

I used to sing Sunday School songs jumping on the bed when I was getting better, also listening to the Soldiers going past down the street, sometimes they would sing as they walked under the street gaslights in the evenings

12yrs old. - November/December time I was taken into Hospital with Bronchial Pneumonia & Pleurisy - laying in the Outpatients on the hospital trolley - I heard them say that I may not last the night.....so, being left on my own in there I prayed to God that He would let me stay to help my Mother with the children. I felt enclosed in His beautiful light and knew that He had heard my prayers and that I would get better. However I was in there for 3 months as it turned into Double Pneumonia and Pleurisy.

I had my 13th. Birthday in there on 24th. December (Christmas Eve 1950) I can still remember that birthday, especially the evening when the nurses and doctors dressed up ready for their Christmas parties. They came around singing Christmas Carols, wishing us a happy Christmas. The party lights shone when they put out the ward lights, it was lovely. The next morning when I woke up there on the bottom of my bed was a Christmas stocking full of gifts. Also there were larger gifts beside my bed. When the nurses came on duty to wash and wake us, they asked when I was going to undo my presents. I said that I would have to wait until my parents or Nanna came because I did not think they could be mine as we would have had no money in our family to pay for such things, also my name was not on them. I had looked at some and put them all back in the Christmas stocking. Matron did the rounds and asked the same thing, she said that Father Christmas had brought them.

But as I had been helping for years to get the Children's stockings ready at home I knew full well that there was no such person. So she agreed that I should wait until someone from the family visited in the afternoon. My father came and I asked him if they were my presents and he said no, that I would have to give them back because we could never pay for them.

Doctor and Matron came to the bed and assured us that they were gifts that had been given to the hospital to be handed out, that I could certainly keep them and take them home. They were the most presents I had ever had for Christmas, there was even some perfume, the others of course I have forgotten but I gave them to my Father to take home for the family and kept the perfume to use while in hospital, also probably a couple of other things like the books and a puzzle to use while there in bed.

Also I was a Girl Guide and used to go to Church at St. Stephen's in Colchester.

Our Girl Guide Caption visited me in hospital and brought me enough wool to knit a cardigan for myself.

I was in the ward for three months hovering between life and death.

When I was able to get out of bed I used to walk around the beds talking to the patients and reading to a blind lady. Sometimes they would put a little child on my bed for me to play with from the nursery, they allowed me to go into the nursery and comfort and sing to the little ones when it was convenient.

After the three months, Jesus healed me enough to go home, where I still had to keep warm and convalesce.

I still like knitting which I learnt when I was about 4yrs old. We didn't have Television or Internet years ago, so time was spent sometimes quietly learning to knit, needlework or reading etc., with our Nanna having patience to teach us.

As a teenager:

I lost a lot schooling through illness

I passed the eleven plus exam and was among the first eleven year olds to go to the New Gilberd School at the North East Essex Technical College and School of Art. Opting to choose to go to a coed and not the selective Girls High School.

Yes I was bullied being from a poor neighbourhood as most were from private homes. No one thought I would pass the Scholarship Exam.

My Parents wondered how they could afford to pay for the uniforms.... so we had a government grant to purchase uniforms. Also tickets for free dinners which was embarrassing standing in line midday for others to know that we were poor.

Some of the schooling I lost was because of a Mastoid painful left ear causing me to have several weeks off School laying in a darkened room at home. Also I had two operations of Polypus on my nose as well of course about the three months previous in hospital with the Pneumonia.

God was with me through all these things and healed me well enough to go back to continue my Education..

***

15yr old. I was confirmed in St. Peter's Anglian Church on North Hill in Colchester. Essex. U.K. Then another long stay in bed diagnosed with Bronchiectasis having to sleep upside down in bed to drain my lungs. While getting better my feet had gone sideways and I could not stand up or walk. I was quite happy staying in bed most of the time as the neighbours used to come and sit and talk with me sometimes and order things from the Mail Order Catalogue that I used to do for my Mother. She bought me a pair of white sandals from the Catalogue hoping to straighten my feet. But they did not work.

Coronation day came for Queen Elizabeth to be crowned and was being broadcast on the radio, so I was determined to go down stairs to listen.

No one was home...my Mother had gone to a friends to watch it on their television. I strapped the white sandals onto my feet - lifted myself out of bed to sit onto the floor - moved to the top of the stairs to go down one step at a time on my bottom, well ! Nanna appeared at the bottom of the stairs looking horrified that I was up there but stayed to watch me come down one step at a time on my bottom and held me up when I reached the last step.

Being able to come down stairs, I spent a lot of time in our front room looking out of the window as people rode their bikes or walked past up and down the road outside our house. They used to wave to me on their way to work or school etc., (One who used to wave became my boyfriend and later my Husband).

Eventually I was able to walk again, Then it was back to school while waiting for an operation on my left lung for the Bronchiectasis.

***

1953.

Boy friend time - We met when I was 15yrs old and Pat 16yrs. in June 1953, we then started going out as boy & girl friends.

Leaving School at 16yrs. old I had a handicap Allowance because I was not well enough to work for quite some time. (I was waiting to have the Lung Operation on my left lung in the Royal Brompton Hospital in London).

The Government allowed me to receive Seven & Sixpence (7/6d) per week..... I thought I was rich because I could buy knitting wool and continue knitting for my young brothers and sisters. A Six Penny Stamp I was able to put in my Saving Book each week. Also I gave my Mother 2/6d. Then would buy a Penny worth of sweets to share with the family.

***

18yrs. old. I was still suffering from Bronchiectasis while waiting for the phone call to go to Brompton Hospital in London regarding the my left Lung. Once there they did a Lower Lobectomy on my left Lung.... that means they cut the lower lobe of it off!

I had thirty nine Stitches around my back and left side, also I was used as a Guinea Pig - for Overlocking Stitching to pull out as one long thread???

Theory & Practice - well - that does not always work. So after 10days when the wound was healing it was time to test by pulling out the thread. However it had all bonded in the skin, so all had to be cut individually to be pulled out!

It took a long time for me to recover. But God was with me all the time..... Convalescence was in the Schiff Home of Recovery for about 3 weeks....before eventually going home.

After all that I had to visit Brompton Hospital in London each year to see the Specialist...At 23yrs old I was pregnant - the Specialist told me they could not heal the Bronchitis that I still had and there was nothing more they could do for me. They said they were so sorry.....but I said God would look after me. And He still does.

1958 Pat and I married in St. James the Less Roman Catholic Church in Colchester. I went to all the lessons about that Religion but stayed Church of England (that is the Anglican Church here in Australia) However I had to agree that if we had Children they would be brought up in the Roman Catholic Church.

My parent's were not happy about that - they would not give permission for us to marry so we had to wait until I was 21yrs. old.

Doctors had advised me not to marry due to medical problems but when you are young and maybe foolish you like to get married the same as your friends.

Pat was in the National Service at the time of the Wedding. So after a brief Holiday (Honeymoon) at a Butlins Holiday Camp, he had to go back to finish his time for the National Service. (In England - Eighteen to 20yr olds had to be in compulsory two year National Service for their Country).

After the wedding we lived with Pat's family. No young person years ago could just move out to a flat or afford a house.

After a while we moved in to live on the top floor of my Aunt Elsie's Café in Wivenhoe before Pat was De mobbed from the Army.

Moving from the Café we were the youngest couple in Essex to buy a house, which we bought in Wivenhoe.

Thanks be to God that we had been working and saving our money.

1968 being pregnant at 3months with my 3rd. baby I was told to have an abortion. Because X-Rays showed Bronchiectasis had come back this time into both lungs. I would not have the baby terminated even due to my health as I believed that God would look after me. It of course was not the best pregnancy having then thrombosis in my legs as well..... I wont go into other details about that.

Our family moved house from Wivenhoe to Brightlingsea .... God looked after me throughout the pregnancy and our baby boy was born in Colchester Maternity Hospital.
  While living in Brightlingsea I started evening classes to learn Oil Painting.
  After a few years we moved to Alresford a nearby Village where I still continued with our Mothers Union and Young Wives Group in Wivenhoe.

***

1973 We Emigrated from Alresford, Essex in England to Perth, Western Australia.

***

Prayer changes everything

EMIGRATED TO AUSTRALIA 1973

We arrived in Perth Western Australia January **1973**. where I had to report to Perth Hospital each year for a chest X ray.

We bought an Orchard in Sawyers Valley in the hills around Perth. After living there for a year and a half decided to move further north due to my ill health where it would be a warmer climate.

1975 we sold the Orchard and came to Carnarvon, there we purchased a Banana Plantation along South River Road. Along the Gascoyne River.

My family were the first people in Australia to make Chocolate Coated Banana's while living on the Plantation.

1975 Mothers Union (M.U. Australia) in Carnarvon I was asked to enroll again because I could not show proof that I was already a member, having helped to start up a Group in Wivenhoe, England about 1962/3. Later I became President of M.U. Carnarvon Branch.

I then started a Caritas Group for young wives at St. George's Anglian Church. Which I did once a week for eight years, mainly for young Mothers and babies.

Testimony of Bootees.

This is my Testimony of Hospital Maternity visiting (re: M.U. Australia). Most Sundays after Church for over 20years visiting young Mum's, taking a gift of card and homemade bootees. Also I had permission to ask The Lord to Bless the new Babies.

I did not touch the babies but put my hand over their little head asking the Lord to bless them. It was lovely to feel the presence of the Holy Spirit gently ministering to them.

I have been a LINK Secretary for a number of years mainly for U.K. plus other M.U. Branches in Australia. At times I have taken turns to be President, Vice President and Treasurer.

I am now a Life Member and Praise The Lord for all He has enabled me to do through M.U. over sixty years. I needed to retire as M.U. President of St. George's Branch in Carnarvon. North Western Australia in January 2023

***

1980 we moved back to Perth, there we bought a house in Forestdale and had a factory at Maddington for making the Chocolate Coated Bananas which we distributed to Deli's and a Supermarket.

Testimony of Healing:

While living there at Forestdale The Lord Healed my Lungs of Bronchiectasis in a Church Service by the laying on of hands by the Bishop who was ministering that Sunday evening.

The healing was not instant, it came about over night.

My Lungs started to bubble and bubbled up more when I lay down to sleep.....so I was frightened to go to sleep and not sure how to lay to get comfortable....

However of course I did go to sleep and in the morning my Lungs had stopped bubbling and the Incurable disease of Bronchiectasis had gone.

It's difficult to say now how I felt, except to say that my lungs were not hurting and that I could breathe much better. So it was much easier to get on with my every day living.

I Praise The Lord Jesus for His healing.

Visit to the Chest Clinic.

Each year a notice used to come for the compulsory X-Ray that I was obliged to have since immigrating here to Australia. It was for a chest X-Ray because of the disease of Bronchiectasis. That last time I had the X-Ray, I went in to see the doctor, who was a neat little Indian Man. He sat across from me the other side of a very large desk. The Doctor asked me lots of details thinking that he had the wrong X-Rays for me.

He went out to ask the Nursing Sister who was on duty regarding the X-Rays if they were the right ones for this patient. He came back after and asked me again what my name was and what I was there for. Also he asked what I had done since my last visit because the disease had disappeared out of my lungs i.e. it was not on the X-Rays.

The lungs were still scarred from the pneumonia's etc., but no Bronchiectasis. He said he wanted to know what I had done as it could possibly help other patients with the same problem because there was no known cure for Bronchiectasis. I told him that I had been on vegetable juices to help heal me. He said that was very good but although they may put the disease in abeyance they could not have taken it away.

So what had I done? - Well I told him that I had gone to Church and had hands laid on for healing asking him not to fall out of the chair laughing! He said he believed me as there was no other way I could have been healed except that God had done it.

Then he said "I want to make sure you are the person you say you are, what about your lobectomy, when did you have that done and where?"

So I told him it was when I was about eighteen years old in The Royal Brompton Hospital in London, U.K.

"Right," he say's "and who did the operation?"
As it was so long ago I said I could not remember. Anyway he said there was no hurry, just to sit still and think for a few moments.

Well I thought and thought then remembered that the Surgeon had a funny name something like Mr. Smelly. He was amazed and said he believed me because he trained under the Surgeon Mr. Smelly in London, in the Royal Brompton Hospital, where I had the operation to remove the lower lobe from my left lung.

This was incredible, a Divine appointment by The Lord.

Praise The Lord that Jesus is our Healer.

The Doctor then told me that I need never to go back for compulsory X-Rays, unless I had any worries about my lungs.

*****

1983 we moved back to Carnarvon on to a Plantation along the River Gascoyne into a small rental house for two and half years. While living there I made our Mothers Union Banner with the help of the Holy Spirit guiding me with the Embroidery.

Also I had my Water Baptism at a Carnarvon Beach, with our Minister and St. George's Anglican Church members.

We had white clothes on and walked up to our knee's in the Indian Ocean before being dunked by the Minister under the water.

It was a once in a lifetime experience to submit ourselves to the Lord.

Afterwards it was good to stand on the beach with the others and family members who had come to share with us. We sang some Praise Songs - then back to the Church hall to change into dry clothes and have a Cuppa.

1985 we were able to purchase our present home here in Carnarvon. Then another incurable disease (Pseudomonas) came into my lungs making me quite ill at times, relying on antibiotics to clear infections. Also I had a stroke down the left side of my body and face - which God healed.

1988 I went back home to England after fifteen years to visit My Mother and family.

While in England --- The Lord allowed me to pray for my young Sister Jasmine for healing of her back.

Here is what happened:

Jasmine's Healing:

Well what happened was this - My Mother, Sister Jill and myself went to visit for Afternoon Tea at my Sister Jasmine and Husband Archie's house.

We knocked at the front door and Archie said we could not see Jasmine as she was in bed with a bad back. I had not seen my sister for fifteen years so asked to visit in her bedroom, Archie said no, she was in too much pain. Anyway I asked - again, please would he ask her if we could visit in her bedroom. Jasmine was very happy we could do that. She had her young baby on the bed so we all stood or sat around. The time before when her back went it took six weeks to heal, so she was prepared to be immobile for most of that time again.

I thought The Lord would like me to pray for healing for her, so quietly I asked her if she would be happy for me to do that. However I needed the room to be cleared of everyone - so I asked Archie to make a Cuppa and everyone to go downstairs for Afternoon tea so I could have time to talk with my sister!

The Lord made the right time for them to leave. Archie took the small child off the bed plus, their two other children, my Mother, Sister Jill plus a next door neighbour who had come in.

Jasmine who could not sit up was happy for me to lay hands on her back, lower down on her spine. She did believe that Jesus is our healer. We had just finished praying when suddenly the door opened and Archie came in with our Afternoon tea. So that was all we could do.

Next morning I phoned to ask how Jasmine was because she had been in so much pain.

One of the children answered the phone and said "wait a minute Auntie Jessie I will get her to come to the phone"

While I was saying "don't disturb her", he had gone.

Then Sister Jasmine was on the phone. I said you should still be in bed resting your back - she said "no - I am up doing the washing , you prayed for healing and Jesus healed me during the night."

Praise the Lord He works in ways we cannot know.

She was so grateful to be up looking after her young family.

The visit was something to treasure.....

***

Here are some other problems and healings that I have received:

Bowel Operation:

Next was a Bowel Operation. It was a blockage in the colon. Things could only come up not down. So after a very frightening night at home alone, the Ambulance picked me up from home and took me into our local Carnarvon Hospital. The next day I was taken down on the Flying Doctor plane for an emergency Operation in a Perth hospital.

I Praise The Lord the Surgeon found that lesions were pressing in on each side of the colon and obstructing the bowel. So they did not have to cut the bowel, only to take off the obstructions and open up that part of the colon.

Eventually I came home where it took about a year to recover and walk comfortably. I am so grateful that God guided the Surgeon and for Jesus healing me again.

Heart Operation:

I had a Heart Operation a few years ago. Once again I was flown down to a Perth Hospital, that time with a heart problem where they diagnosed a leaking vein and had to operate. They cauterized the leaking vein by going up to the heart through my groin. Then I was able to stay in Perth with family to be near the hospital for check-ups, until I was able to fly home again.

It was marvelous not to have all the chest pains that had been going on for years due to the leaking vein, which had been difficult to diagnose without the latest technology.

Once again to Praise the Lord for His healing.

Antibiotics:

I was allowed to keep antibiotic's at home for whenever I would get an infection in my lungs to start taking them. A few years ago being on them constantly the Dr. said next time don't start them and we will do further investigations, because soon there would be none to fall back on.

I was quite upset when I came home and asked The Lord about healing.

Nothing happened so I stood in the lounge room and shouted out Kill Pseudomonas and I believed The Holy Spirit said "Google it" !

Well I wasn't sure if it was a good idea but I googled it and read that the only herb that would kill pseudomonas was Oregano.

Praise The Lord - I started to drink a small amount in tea form each day to help keep my lungs free of infection and I did not need antibiotic's for nearly two years. ....

How about that? It was the longest time that I had gone without antibiotics for many years.

It was a real blessing from The Lord God.

Other problems are or have been:

Arthritis, Gallbladder trouble, Osteoarthritis, Asthma etc.,

Torn Ligament

Jesus recently healed me of a Torn Ligament in my left leg. I was staying with family about 600klms. from my home where I knocked my leg very hard against some wooden furniture.

My adult granddaughter and her five year old took me to Hospital where they wheeled me around in a wheel chair (it was too painful to walk).
    The Hospital diagnosed a Torn Ligament so the Physio gave me a special shoe, leg bandage, plus walking stick.

I stayed with my family with leg raised for a week until I was able to be taken back to my own home.

After the Physio saying ("it could never heal"), Jesus healed the torn ligament completely.

It has been really marvellous to walk with no pain in that place.

I continue to be thankful.

***

Year 2021/23

Most of the year 2021 was painful, I was in and out of hospital with back pains from my spine (scoliosis) plus chest problems, mainly coming from my Gall bladder. End of November 2021 I was flown down by The Flying Doctor plane again to a Perth Hospital where they took a week getting my heart, lungs and body well enough to be operated on.

Eventually Dec. 4th. 2022 I was able to be well enough to have a Gallbladder Operation. With only 40% lung capacity it was going to be a bit tricky as I was so ill they took a chance and it worked out alright.

A few days after the operation my heart went into Atrial Fibrillation, I thought I would never see home again. I contracted a lung infection in hospital also fluid on the lungs which they treated with Antibiotics.

But The Lord was with me in all this. Eventually with the expertize of the marvellous Medical Staff I was able to be released from Hospital.

My Daughter collected me from the Hospital. We stayed a week in the City waiting for a plane to fly us to my home 1,000klms. north. She was my Carer for about nine months. My Daughter left 26th. of April 2023 returning to her home over 1,000klms down South.

She left knowing I would able to fend for myself with help from family who live in Town for shopping etc.,

I thank The Lord that she was able to look after me as I was unable move much when we first arrived home.

I needed a special chair, walking stick, also a wheel walker to regain muscle that I had lost over the year. I was then only weighing 47kilos.

My healing is still ongoing but am able to get on with life now and can thank The Lord for bringing me through the most dreadful time.

Prayer changes everything

Car Problem. Angel in disguise?

Four ladies (one was myself) were on our way back from a Ministry meeting further north, we were driving about four hours from our home, when suddenly the car engine started spluttering. Well, we could see steam coming out of the front of the car.

So we pulled over and came to a stop along the side of the road. No other vehicles were in sight as it was a long lonely stretch of road.

We opened the car bonnet to let things cool down and did not know what to do.

Then we decided it would be best as Christian's to pray and ask The Lord for help.

After a while waiting in the heat of the day about 30 to 40 deg. Celsius, in the distance we saw a car coming towards us and hoped that the driver would stop and help us.

We praised The Lord that the driver pulled along side and asked if we were alright.

After explaining what had happened, he kindly looked under the bonnet and said that things were not good. He said he would try to fix it. After he did what he did he advised us to drive slowly to the next left hand road turn off to a farm house. Then to phone for our family to pick us up and arrange for a mechanic to come.

We thanked him, he would not take any payment and said he must be going. We noted that his toolbox was very old also his vehicle and wondered who he was. I don't remember him saying his name but as soon as we got back in the car he was gone.

The next story is taken from my book... 'True Stories of God'

It is a testimony of how God can use The Holy Spirit through us as Christians.

Cruise Ship Story.

While my husband and myself were on this large Cruise Ship, most days I would take my Bible and knitting after our Buffet Breakfast, then find a quiet spot to do my Bible Reading.

One morning an older lady came to sit and ask me if I was a Christian or what religion was I, because she recognized that it was a Bible I was reading.

So, yes I told her I was a Christian and after talking for a while she asked if I would pray for her young Grandson who had been diagnosed with cancer and was very ill.

I did tell her that maybe she should pray for him but she said she couldn't as she was not sure if God would hear her prayers.

Then I said 'Yes of course I will pray for him'. Feeling happy about that, off she went to look for her husband who was wandering around the ship.

A few days later they found my husband and myself one evening sitting having a drink. Then Phil (the lady who had approached me regards praying) asked if they could join us with a drink in the large bar area of the Ballroom where we were sitting. There was a stage with a live show going on that we were watching at the time when they found us there.

Apparently they had been able to phone home and was told their Grandson was a lot better, so they wanted to thank me for the prayers I had prayed for him.

Then she looked at me and suddenly said "I want what you have". I asked her "What do you mean" and she said "You know" So I said "No, I have no idea what you mean". So we repeated all this again, then she came out with the words "I want what you have in there" touching me in the middle of my chest she said "I want Jesus in me"

Well what a surprise, especially sitting in the noisy area where people were having a drink with their friends while watching a live performance on the stage.

So I suggested we go down to her cabin, there I could lead her in the 'Sinners Prayer' to invite Jesus into her life.
    We left our husbands in the ballroom/theatre with their drinks, talking to each other during an interval in the show.

Then in Phil and Bert's cabin we sat down and I asked Phil why she had decided to have Jesus permanently in her life?

"Well" she said most of her family were Christians and she was not sure how to be one, she asked me to explain how.

I said that people need to repent of the wrong things they had done in their life and really mean they are sorry and ask Jesus to forgive their sins and come into their heart - then they are born again into the Kingdom of God.

Here is an example of the Sinners Prayer;

Dear Jesus I know I am a sinner I repent of my sins, I do believe that you died on the Cross even for me.
Please forgive me and come into my heart to take charge of my life.
Thank you that you are now Lord of my life.
I also acknowledge God as my Heavenly Father and accept your Holy Spirit....
Amen.

Of course there different ways to pray the Sinners Prayer but this is what it is all about to become a Christian.

*

If you pray the Sinners Prayer and really mean it
you are
immediately accepted by Jesus.

You are Born Again in the Spirit and belong to
the Kingdom of God, Our Heavenly Father.

You need to tell a Christian that you have taken
this step.

To speak out is an act of faith and confirms that
you have now become a Christian.

Then to begin reading the Bible -
St. John: Chapter 3 verse 16.

Is a good place to start if you decide to do this.

It says:-

(For God so loved the world that he gave his one
and only Son, that whoever believes in him shall
not perish but have eternal life.)

May God Bless You with His Love.

Back to Phil in the Cabin -

I said to her if she would like to I could lead her in the Sinners Prayer and that she could repeat it with me - if she really did mean that she wanted Jesus in her life.

Now this lady was over eighty years old and I had never ministered to someone this age on my own - in a cabin on a Cruise Ship in the middle of the ocean!

Phil decided to sit comfortably on the small settee and I sat on a chair facing her holding her hands as we began to pray. She repeated after me the prayer to invite Jesus in, then I let go of her hands - laid my hands on her and asked for a special infilling of the Holy Spirit as she had asked me to.

Then all was quiet while I sat back down and waited for her to say something, then the tears started to fall, just running down her face.

When I asked if she was alright she just nodded and sat there with a look of absolute peace on her face.

Eventually after what seemed ages, she said that she felt all brand new, that all her troubles had gone away and a big weight had gone from her.

Phil believed that Jesus was with her and insisted that she was not crying.

I explained that all the tears were washing her clean from the sins that had been in her life.

The whole cabin throughout this time had been filled with a wonderful peace.

So after all that, we went back up to join our husbands who were still watching the show.

Phil's face was beaming and they wondered what we had been doing?

Phil told Bert she would tell him later.!

Well a few days after this lady Phil found me on the ship in the same place as before with Pat my husband and said "Bert wants the same".

"What do you mean?" I asked. - She said "You know what I mean".

Well once again I didn't have a clue what she was talking about - eventually she said "Bert wants Jesus".

What a lovely surprise for a man in his eighties to ask his wife to ask me to do the same for him as I had for Phil.

I told her that she could lead Bert in the Prayer like I did for her now that she was a Christian but of course she was not confident at that time to do it.

Also she told me that since she had asked for Prayer for her young Grandchild he was beginning to recover from the cancer even quicker - they had been keeping in contact on the phone from the ship like I had already mentioned.

I had told Phil that as she was now a Christian, Jesus would hear her prayers. She had told Bert this, so he wanted to make sure of the same, that Jesus would hear his prayers.

The other thing that was very important to them both was to know that they would be in Heaven when their earthly bodies died. Because they were both over eighty years old.

So how did we minister then to Bert?

We decided to take Bert down to their cabin and pray for him there, similar to the prayers we prayed for Phil.

We sat him on a chair, not on the settee, so that I could ask Phil to stand with me as we placed our hands on his shoulders to pray the sinners prayer with him.

Well he found it hard to hear what we were saying - so it took a while to repeat everything for him but we did it!

Nothing dramatic happened but he was sure that he had invited Jesus into his life and repented of his sins.

He seemed quite happy about this so we went back up to join Pat who was in the ballroom watching the live show with other friends that we had made on the cruise ship.

A few days later we disembarked, so Pat helped Phil and Bert with their luggage.

As Pat walked along the pavement helping Phil, Bert came beside me and said these words:

"You didn't think I was dinkum did you?"

Well what could I say apart from the fact that I was not sure that he had heard alright.

He assured me he had heard and touching the centre of his chest as we walked along he said "He is in here and has been hearing my prayers".

Bert was very positive about that and so pleased that he had become a Christian even in his eighties.

He had been going to Church with his family for many years but had never thought to ask Jesus to be Lord of his life.

Bert and Phil went back to their home in Adelaide and we back to our home in Perth, Western Australia.

A few weeks (maybe a few months) later we received a letter from Phil thanking us for the prayers and saying that their grandson was well. Praise The Lord that He sees us wherever we are, even on a Cruise Ship in the middle of the Ocean and allows His Holy Spirit to work through us to help bring people into Salvation.

Amen.

We cannot hide from God our Heavenly Father. That can be a great comfort to us knowing that:

> The Holy spirit of Jesus
> is always with us.

Testimony of Third Baby.

Knowing that I should not be having another baby I waited until I was three months pregnant before going to the Doctors.

Already having two babies one in 1960 and one in 1964 against Doctors orders Because I did not believe in abortions.

Now there we were again.

So when I did go to the Doctor he said that this time I most definitely would need an abortion due to my health because the chest X-ray showed that the Bronchiectasis had returned not only in the remaining part of the left lung but was now in the right lung as well.

He explained that it would get much worse as the pregnancy developed by pushing up the lungs and contracting them more.

After praying about it I decided that God would look after me as I could not bear to kill the baby.

For most of the pregnancy therefore I was very ill, coughing up sputum, pain in the lungs and thrombosis in my legs. Also asthma, Arthritis and Hay fever.

Having my husband and two young daughters to look after I was on quite a lot of medication to cope with our every day living and having to rest quite a bit each day.

My husband took me to the maternity home when the baby seemed to be on the way but it was a false alarm, so we had to wait another week before he was born.

It was a risky birth with me on some sort of breathing gas, therefore the baby went to sleep halfway through the birth cannel.

Eventually Praise The Lord our Son was born perfectly well. Then I was taken back into the ward.

When the nurse came and gave me the baby to breast feed I said she had given me the wrong one. She was very cross with me and said to get on and feed it. - as I would not do that she called in the Matron who said how did I think it was not my child.?

I told Matron that I had watched him being born and knew that was not his face.

As there were two surnames the same, she went away and came back with the two Larman babies and asked me to say which was mine.

I said it was a boy and pointed to one of them. She uncovered them and unwrapped the nappies - yes I was right because the other was a girl which they had given me to feed.

I was told that I could sue the hospital for this but no, I was so glad that The Lord had delivered my son safely and that the other Mother had the correct baby girl.

I praise The Lord for all His help.

Also while I was there I had an operation to have my tubes tied, so no chance of having another pregnancy.

I give thanks to The Lord that we did not abort the baby and for allowing me to have a Son. Amen.

Testimony of Healing on the way.

After Church morning tea the congregation were leaving to go home.

It was our Tourist Season, as they were leaving a husband and wife stopped me to say goodbye. The wife then asked if I would pray for her husband who had Emphysema and was quite ill with it. It was about a six hour drive to go home and they thought he would have to go into hospital when they arrived there.

Well yes, I did lay hands on him and asked The Lord for healing for him. They thanked me although nothing special seemed to happen at that time.

About a week later I received a letter from them saying they were so excited that on the drive home they believed the Holy spirit presence was in the car with them and that her husband was healed on the drive home.

Sometimes we have to wait on the Lord for His Special Timing.

What a lovely Testimony they could share with their family and friends.

Praise the Lord.

***

Salvation Testimony

At sixty nine years old my Husband Pat was diagnosed with acute Myeloid Leukemia. He had been ill for a long time but suddenly has this diagnosis which he found it hard to cope with. Refusing the treatment offered except the ones for pain of course, he gradually got worse.

I was his carer for six months as he would not have anyone else come into help when he really needed it.

To cut a long story short - when he was mostly bedridden on oxygen and refused to go into hospital I was still looking after him.

One night as I was settling him into bed, I put the oxygen on for the night and made him comfortable on the pillows, by this time he could hardly speak. So he held onto my hand and wanted me to stay.

I was standing by the bed and after a while I said that I could not stand any longer and kissed him goodnight. - He would not let go of my hand still. He was not a Christian so I said why don't you give Jesus a go, ask Him for help to come into our heart.

Well suddenly he shot right up in the bed, put his arms out and in a loud voice shouted "alright Jesus you can come in" Then collapsed back onto the pillows.

I stood there quite shaken by the loud voice, then Praised The Lord that he had done it.! However he found a bit more voice and told me to get out, realizing what he had done.

So I sat in the lounge room very shaken up but praised The Lord that Pat had come into Salvation and would go to Heaven when he died.

The Lord God was Gracious and three days later took him home to Heaven at 4am on January 21st. 2007.

We had been married since 1958 when we were 21years old, having met up as fifteen year olds.

I was still at College and Pat had finished school and was in an apprenticeship for Plumbing.

His National Service for the Army was deferred until he finished his apprenticeship as a 20year old.

Pat was still in the Army when we married.

Visitation

As a four or five year old child, Nanna tucked me into her big bed for the night. (My Mother myself and my younger sister lived with Nanna while my Father was in the Army).

Often I shared Nannas big bed if I was not very well.

That night after tucking me in and leaving the small night candle alight, she left me and went down stairs for the evening.

Laying awake for a while I saw Auntie Gladys standing in the doorway in her nightdress. She said she had come to say 'Goodnight' then she left and I sent to sleep.

Waking up in the morning I asked Nanna where Auntie Gladys had slept and if she was up having breakfast with them.
She said "no she wasn't there, why did I think that she was" I told her that she had come to say goodnight before I went to sleep.

Well my poor Nanna realized something must have happened. She got ready and walked a long way to their house at the end of the pathway by the Hythe River.
Where she found her brother Mick, Gladys husband beside himself in tears that his wife Gladys had died that night.

We had no phones years ago or transport so Nanna had to walk, she never rode a bike.

Praise The Lord this was His way to let her know about her Sister-in-law and that she was obedient to listen and understand my Visitation.

Thank you Lord.

A Voice

Living in Australia on an Orchard in Sawyers Valley which is up in the Hills around the City of Perth, I used to go to the little wooden Church in Mount Helena.

That particular Sunday I went on my own as my family must have been busy doing something else.

As I was walking down the aisle with wooden pews each side, about half way down a voice said "Clara died"

I stood still and looked around but no one was near me to say anything.

So I found a seat and knelt down to pray and asked The Lord for confirmation if it was my Aunt Clara in England that had died.

A few days later an air mail letter came from my Nanna in England (Clara's sister) telling me that my Auntie Clara had gone to Heaven.

That was the confirmation that I needed in regard to the voice that said (Clara died)

> The Lord works in mysterious ways His wonders
> to perform.

Baby in Pram.

Years ago sitting outside a shop in our Village in England, my cousin's wife asked if I would look after her baby son who was sitting up in his pram.

It was one of those lovely big English prams. Of course I said yes and sat on the seat next to the pram while she went in to get her shopping.

As I sat looking and talking to the beautiful baby his face took on a lovely out of this world look. He looked as I thought he could have been an Angel Child, his face just glowed.

It was a special moment in time and all was back to normal when the Mother came out of the shop.

It was during that night that The Lord took the child home to Heaven.

All the family were so distressed but I was never able to let them know what I had seen.

However it has remained in my memory even after all these years.

Sometimes The Lord God allows us to see His Glory in part, although we cannot understand somethings at the time what it really means.

Letter to God

Dear Lord God,
Please teach me to Pray.
As long as I live I need to Pray.

But my Prayers must be right so that your
Will, will be done.

I need to be more righteous, as it says in the
Bible -

"...The effectual Fervent Prayer of a righteous
man availeth much"
James: Chapter 5 verse 16

Also I need faith, even as small as a Mustard
Seed,
so that my Prayers will remove Mountains -
Mountains of doubt & fear, sickness, ill health,
bondages & pride.

Otherwise my Prayers will not be as effective
as they need to be.

Cont'd.....on next page.

Dear Lord God,

I need to Pray through Jesus Christ my Lord,
Your Son who died on the Cross
for the sin of the world including mine.

Dear Lord God,
I know also that I need your Holy Spirit to
help me to Pray.
Please allow Him to teach me to Pray real
effective Prayers.
So that your Will can be done on earth
through the Prayers that I pray.

Let them not be selfish Prayers from my soul
but Prayers from my Spirit in line with the
teaching in your

Holy Bible.

Amen.

....

Taken from my book 'Godly Verses'

Computer in the House?

For a few years at the works Christmas Party I sat with one of the women, she knew that I was a Christian so she used to ask me to pray for her. This went on for a few years other than that I did not know her very well.

Then one day in the morning she knocked on my front door in an agitated state asking if I had a computer in the house?

Why did she want to know that, she wouldn't say, so I asked if she would like to come in but would only do so if I agreed to show her the computer.

Well I did as she asked and invited her to stay and have a cup of tea.

She sat crying in my lounge room while I made the Cuppa.

When she was able to talk she said she had a dream and that she was to visit me, to talk to me if I had a computer.

She was not sure where I lived apart from which road in town, so as she travelled slowly along the road her car stopped in front of my house.

That was how she was standing on the door step asking if I had a computer.

Previously at the parties over the years I had witnessed to her that she needed Jesus in her life.

I was able to tell her that probably was the reason why she was there.

Having said that, she started crying again and said she needed help but was not keen to accept Jesus at that time.

However after a bit more talking she was convinced to accept Jesus and repent of any sins. The Holy spirit of course was with me organizing all this.

Afterwards she reported to our Minister what had happened he blessed her and welcomed her into our Church.

She became a lovely Christian woman being a great asset to our Church for many years.

I praise The Lord for allowing me to be used for His Glory and His will to be done at that particular time.

If you are not already a Christian,
here is a Prayer for you to pray to become one.

TO BE A CHRISTIAN

Dear Jesus I know I am a sinner I repent of
my sins, please forgive me and come in to
my heart to take charge of my life.
Thank you.
You are now Lord of my life,
I also acknowledge God as Father and accept
your Holy Spirit...Amen.

...

If you pray the above Prayer and really mean
it you are immediately accepted by Jesus.
You are Born Again and belong to the Kingdom of God. You need to tell a Christian
that you have taken this step, to speak out is
an action of faith and confirms that you have
now become a Christian.
You need to begin reading the Bible.
St. John: Chapter 3 verse 3. Says:
Jesus declared, "I tell you the truth,
no-one can see the Kingdom of God
unless he is born again."

...

(May God Bless You With His Love.)

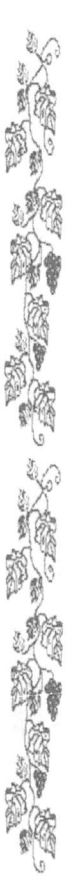

Here is a version of The Lords Prayer.

Most versions differ from each other but the meaning is always the same, this is the way that I particularly like to pray this Prayer.

From St. Luke: Chapter 11 verse 2
in your Holy Bible.

Our Father who art in Heaven,

Hallowed be your Name.

Your Kingdom come. Your Will be Done.

On Earth as it is in Heaven

Give us today our daily bread.

And Forgive us our Trespasses, as

We Forgive those who sin against us.

Lead us not into Temptation

But Deliver us from evil.

For Yours is the Kingdom,

The Power and The Glory,

For Ever and Ever - Amen.

The Lords Prayer is very special it covers everything we need to pray for.

The Prayer on the next page is taken from my 'Book of Prayers'
Available from the Amazon site.

Pray for Lost Souls.

I know that your heart grieves God for all those lost souls who have not come to the knowledge and love of Jesus yet.

I pray Lord God that you will allow your Holy Spirit to move around them to somehow soften their hard hearts towards you.

I pray today that Christians will be able to speak out of the love of Jesus so that those who are not saved will indeed begin to wonder what they are missing out on.

I pray that today many souls will come into Salvation through out the world.

Help us as Christians to reach out to those who are in the world, help us to reach out with love, joy and peace to whoever you bring before us today.

May your signs and miracles continue through out the world as a sure witness that Jesus is alive, that He lives for ever and ever with you God Our Father in Heaven.

Bless all who come before us today God, also please bless me so that I too can be a blessing for others.

Amen.

Just an Update for this Little Book.

Middle of the year 2022 at home morning time, I phoned for an Ambulance to take me to our Local Hospital. The Ambulance Crew were very good as they had taken me in a few times before.

I had dreadful pains in my chest and back, so was given some medication as I was too painful for them to move me.

Once in the hospital they did numerus tests as to how best to treat me.

The Diagnosis found many things wrong: Gallbladder pain, Atrial Fibrillation, Asthma, Bronchitis, Scoliosis, with two vertebra - one near the bottom of the spine and one near the top of the spine, each had moved causing terrible back pain.

They put me on a lot of medication and I was flown down on the Flying Doctor Plane to a Perth hospital in the City about 1,000 kilometres away from Carnarvon.

Two Surgeons refused to operate on my Gall Bladder as they said it was too risky to remove it. Another one said he would operate if my body could be stabilized with the 50% lung capacity that I had.

The Anesthetist checked me out and found that I only had 40% lung capacity but she said she would sit with me and go carefully with the anesthetic if they could operate.

It took another week for the Doctors to stabilize my body to be able to operate.

Then my body developed a lung infection. The Doctor said they could not start antibiotic's before a surgery.

They explained there was not much chance of me coming through the operation to remove the Gallbladder and asked if I still would like to go ahead with it.

However I said "please go ahead" as I could no longer bear all the terrible pain hoping at least the Gallbladder pain would be gone and that God would look after me.

I Praise The Lord that I came through the Keyhole surgery for the infected Gallbladder and they started straightway with a drip of antibiotics.

After a few days continuing to get better, the morning my daughter was coming to pick me up to be discharged my heart went into very strong Atrial Fibrillation with not much oxygen going to my lungs.

Suddenly three Surgeons appeared at the bottom my bed with their entourage not knowing how best to start with all heart, lungs and all the other things wrong with my body including dreadful pain from my spine. I was in a big mess!

As I could not be moved they brought an Ex Ray machine to my bed, took blood tests, gave me pain medication etc.,

I Praised The Lord the Gallbladder had been removed successfully and prayed to recover from whatever was happening at that time.

All the Doctors, Nurses, everyone, treated me very well by masking the pain and looking after me. Eventually I was able to be discharged from hospital with my daughter coming to collect me who was to be my Carer.

I had lost so much weight only weighing 48 kilos and was just about skin and bone.

After a week in Perth waiting for a flight we were able to fly the 1,000klms. home where my daughter continued to be my Carer. I could not do much to look after myself, could not even make a cup of tea.

The Physiotherapist from our hospital in Carnarvon would come to our house to give me exercise's to start me getting my body moving again. I had lost the muscles in my arms and could not lift much to get them back again. Plus I could hardly stand up without holding on to something.

My daughter who had retired from work was able to stay until I was able to fend for myself which took the best part of a year. I am able now to have a walker, walking stick and can drive my car but have to sit on a cushion as I lost about 3" in height due to curvature of the Spine and could not see over the steering wheel of the car!

At the moment I am well enough to continue with Computer work and some Art work. Stopping now and then to relieve some of the aches and pains of course but am so gratefull to start getting on with life once more. My family help with shopping as am not able yet to do that but am very well looked after even living on my own once more.

I could not have come through any of this without The Lord God, Jesus His Son and the Holy spirit. Through all this the Holy Spirit has been with me and took away all fear. Praise The Lord God that He is still healing me day by day.
    I am so glad that I invited Jesus into my life as a five year old child. So I have grown up with Jesus doing many miracles in my life.

Amen

November. 2023.

Now I have been struck with Shingles down the left side of my chest. At times the pain is so bad it is just about unbearable, also I was told that it may take up to three to five weeks to heal.

I am thankful to The Lord for all the medication I am allowed to help me cope with the excruciating pain, plus masking cream and hot pack to lay on my painful side.

Thankfully in January the Shingles left, so I am not in that awful pain. Praise The Lord.

***

I do Praise The Lord for all His
Blessings towards me.
Amen.

Scripture quotations are taken from the HOLY BIBLE,
NEW INTERNATIONAL VERSION.
Copyright © 1973,1978,1984 by International Bible Society
Also: From the Authorised King James Version

.....

Copyright of this Book
'My Little Book of Testimonies'
Writings
&
Illustrations belong to the Author:
Jessie M.R. Larman

A catalogue record for this
book is available from the
National Library of Australia

ISBN: 978-0-6450891-8-9 (paperback)
ISBN: 978-0-6450891-9-6 (ebook)

www.ingramcontent.com/pod-product-compliance
Lightning Source LLC
Chambersburg PA
CBHW071848290426
44109CB00017B/1975